VROOM!
Speed and Acceleration

Stephanie Paris

Consultants

Timothy Rasinski, Ph.D.
Kent State University

Lori Oczkus
Literacy Consultant

Katie McKissick
Physical Science Consultant

Based on writing from
TIME For Kids. TIME For Kids and the *TIME
For Kids* logo are registered trademarks of
TIME Inc. Used under license.

Publishing Credits

Dona Herweck Rice, *Editor-in-Chief*
Lee Aucoin, *Creative Director*
Jamey Acosta, *Senior Editor*
Heidi Fiedler, *Editor*
Lexa Hoang, *Designer*
Stephanie Reid, *Photo Editor*
Rane Anderson, *Contributing Author*
Rachelle Cracchiolo, *M.S.Ed., Publisher*

Image Credits: pp.8–9, 18 (bottom), 30
(left) Associate Press; p.26 (bottom) Warden
and Scholars of New College, Oxford/The
Bridgeman Art; p.27 (top) The Stapleton
Collection/The Bridgeman Art; p.43 (top)
California Institute of Technology; pp.34, 44,
48, 51 (bottom) Getty Images; pp.30 (right),
36 (bottom), 47, 49 (both), 50 (right), 51 (top),
52–53 (bottom) 56 (left), 59 (bottom)
iStockphoto; p.52 Science Source &
iStockphoto; p.31 (top) NASA; p.7 (center)
NASA/JPL-Caltech; p.5 (bottom) epa/Newscom;
p.19 (top) Modesto Bee/Newscom; pp.13
(bottom), 50 (left) REUTERS/Newscom; pp.10–
11, 14–15, 23, 33, 38–39, 54–55 (illustrations)
Kevin Panter; p.32 Martin Bond/Photo
Researchers, Inc.; p.35 Laima Druskis/Science
Source; p.25 (bottom) Royal Institution of Great
Britain/Science Source; p.12 Corbis/SuperStock;
All other images from Shutterstock.

Teacher Created Materials

5301 Oceanus Drive
Huntington Beach, CA 92649-1030
http://www.tcmpub.com
ISBN 978-1-4333-4938-6
© 2013 Teacher Created Materials, Inc.

Table of Contents

What Is Speed?

Race cars zoom across the finish line, soccer balls whiz down the field, and dancers throw themselves through the air in leaps and bounds. Moving fast feels exhilarating, but how fast is fast? Kyle Petty, a record-winning race-car driver, sums it up well. "**Speed** is **relative**. Does it feel fast going 70 miles per hour down an 8-lane highway? No, probably not, but I bet it does if you are going down some single-lane dirt road. It's the same in a race car. It depends on the track." In other words, how fast something is moving depends on what it's being compared to. The fastest car appears as slow as a turtle when it's being compared to the fastest jet, but how fast is a jet when it's compared to the speed of light?

Bicycle: 81 miles per hour

Car: 267 miles per hour

The Fastest

Airplane: 2,200 miles per hour

Spaceship: 39,000 miles per hour

THINK LINK

- What does it mean to go fast?
- What affects how fast or slow an object moves?
- How can we speed up or slow down a moving object?

Light Speed

Light travels at about 186,000 miles per second. Scientists believe this is the fastest anything in our universe can travel.

How long does it take you to walk to school? The answer depends on two things: the distance you need to travel and how quickly you are moving. Speed is a way to measure how fast something is going. It is defined as a change of position over time. It describes how long it takes for something to get from one place to another.

Physics Facts

Physicists are scientists who study the universe. They use math to understand and explain why things move and change the way they do.

Stargazer

Physicist Amy Mainzer is an expert on asteroids and galaxies. She's the deputy project scientist for the Wide-Field Infrared Survey Explorer (WISE) mission, which uses an advanced telescope. She's a Harry Potter fanatic and loves math, skating, and most importantly, her job.

Measuring Speed

The point of a race is to determine who or what moves the fastest. That's exactly what some kids do each year in derbies. In these races, participants start with the same materials. They begin with a block of wood, an **axle**, and wheels, or they might use a small plastic model car. Either way, only one car can win the race.

In a race, each participant's car travels on the same track at the same time. The winner is easy to spot. Just look for the car that crosses the finish line first. But what if you want to compare the race times of your school's winner with another school's winner? You wouldn't need to race them side by side. All you would need to do is compare their speeds.

Speed is described as *distance per time*. This can be measured in miles per hour, meters per second, or millimeters per year. The measurement you use depends on what you are measuring.

Usain Bolt

Fast Formula

In 2012, Usain Bolt of Jamaica broke a new record by running 100 meters in 9.63 seconds. How many meters can Usain Bolt run in 1 second? Use this fast formula, where *S* is speed, *D* is distance, and *T* is time:

$$S = \frac{D}{T}$$

$$? = \frac{100 \text{ meters}}{9.69 \text{ seconds}}$$

$$\frac{10.3 \text{ meters}}{1 \text{ second}} \times 1 \text{ second} = 10.3 \text{ meters}$$

Units of Measurement

Imagine pushing a toy car along a track. With one strong push, the car zips down the 2-meter track in 1 second. The toy is moving at a speed of 2 meters per second. Now imagine a real car. It zooms down the highway and travels 60 miles in 1 hour. It is going 60 miles per hour.

2 meters

It makes sense to describe the real car in miles since it is traveling such large distances so quickly.

1 mile = 1609.344 meters

What if we described the toy car in miles per hour and the real car in meters per second? It turns out the toy car is going about 4.47 miles per hour. The real car is going 26.82 meters per second. You can express speed using any distance and time.

1 second

1 hour

60 miles

Velocity

Imagine a girl strapping on her skates for a big race. She gets set, the whistle blows, and the racers are off! She is going much faster than any of the others. She glides along the track, passes the judges, and continues on through the astonished audience, who jumps out of her way. Then, she skates right out the door, forgetting one important step. She never crossed the finish line! Another much slower racer crosses the finish line and wins the race. Why? The faster racer was going the wrong way! Sometimes, speed isn't the only thing that matters—direction is important, too. **Velocity** is speed plus direction.

Kicking It up a Notch

Almost every sport relies on velocity. Athletes must hit, kick, or throw a ball at the right speed and in the right direction. They must move their bodies quickly and accurately across the field and catch the ball in time. The game depends on the speed and the direction the players move in.

Hi-Tech Velocity

Does your favorite electronic game involve dodging fireballs or jumping on platforms? Do you have to fling birds or shoot lasers at just the right angle and moment? Then your game relies on velocity!

Back and Forth

Velocity is speed measured in a specific direction. Velocity works the same way with cars, spaceships, and galaxies as it does with humans. This person's velocity changes as he changes speeds and changes directions. Here, traveling to the right is a form of positive velocity. Traveling to the left is negative velocity.

maximum speed = 3 meters per second

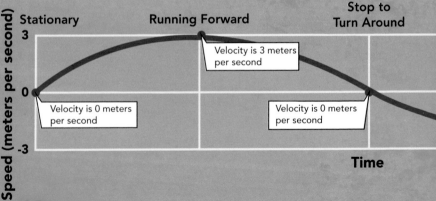

Stationary

Running Forward

Stop to Turn Around

Velocity is 3 meters per second

Velocity is 0 meters per second

Velocity is 0 meters per second

Speed (meters per second)

3

0

-3

Time

STOP! THINK...

- What would the graph look like if the character ran forward the entire time?

- What velocity does the man have when he is standing still?

- Why is the velocity expressed as -3 when the man runs backward?

Running Backward

Stationary

Velocity is 0 meters per second

Velocity is -3 meters per second

Going Faster

What makes things go? And how can we make them go faster? Every object has many forces acting on it. **Gravity** pulls down. The ground pushes up. A shove can push something forward, and **friction** may slow it down.

An object needs **energy** to move. To move fast, all that energy needs to be pushing in the same direction. The trick to making an object go faster is to maximize the forces that make it go and minimize the forces that hold it back. Think about the forces that help a model car speed up or slow down. Where does the car's energy come from? Can you think of ways to modify the car so the forces making it go faster have a stronger impact than the ones slowing it down?

Tinker's Tip

Imagine a model car without wheels. The race begins, the gate lifts, and although the car may move forward a little, it's definitely not going to win the race! The force of friction slowing the car is stronger than the force of gravity pulling it toward the bottom of the track.

Rapid Descent

Downhill skiers try to maximize their downward force while minimizing the friction holding them back. But they must also keep safety in mind. These skiers often travel at speeds exceeding 80 miles per hour! Their skis and clothes are designed to minimize friction and help protect them in case of a crash.

Power Up

Energy is the ability to do work and make changes. There are two major kinds of energy. **Potential energy** is energy that is stored or that results from position. Nothing is changing yet, but the energy is ready and waiting to be used. A car resting at the top of a hill has potential energy.

Kinetic energy is working energy. As the car zooms down the track, the kinetic energy is the amount of work necessary to get it from its stopped position to its full velocity.

On the Track

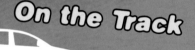

At the Top

Model cars at the top of a racetrack demonstrate potential energy. When they are released, their energy is released as well, and they zoom down the track!

On an Incline

Cars traveling down an incline use kinetic energy. There are two main forces at work. Gravity pulls the cars toward the ground, and friction slows their progress.

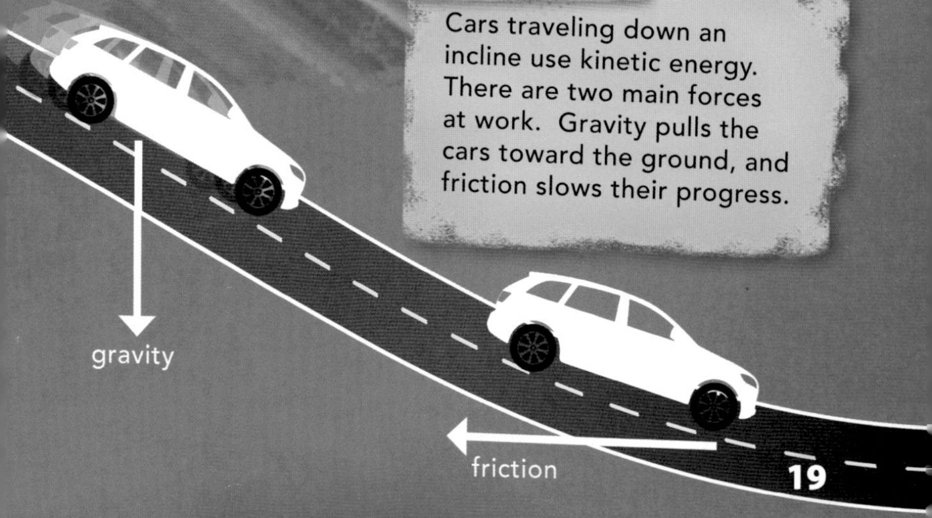

gravity

friction

Built for Speed

Racers work hard to make their cars go as fast as possible. But in nature, moving fast isn't a game. It's a matter of survival. Animals that hunt need to be able to chase down their prey. Every second counts in the wild. Some car designers set out to model cars after speedy animals. Sometimes, the car resembles the animal's shape. Other times, the car is named after the animal that inspired it.

Jaguar

Chevrolet Impala

Shelby Cobra

Dodge Ram

Fastest on Land

The cheetah holds the title as the fastest animal on land. For short bursts, it can race after prey at 65 to 70 miles per hour. It can go from 0 to 60 miles per hour in 3 seconds! It has large lungs and nostrils that take in oxygen quickly to send to its muscles as it runs. Its claws stick out to create **traction**. And its flat tail helps it make sharp turns easily.

Ups and Downs

Things don't just start off going fast, build speed, and then stop instantly. Like the cheetah that takes 3 seconds to get from 0 to 60 miles per hour, objects also need time to speed up and slow down. That's where **acceleration** comes into play. Acceleration is a change in velocity over time. When something accelerates, it speeds up or changes direction. **Deceleration** describes something that is slowing down, which can also be called *negative acceleration*. Whenever you have something that is going fast, you will eventually need it to stop. The ability to control acceleration and deceleration is important for toys, cars, animals, spacecrafts, and pretty much everything else!

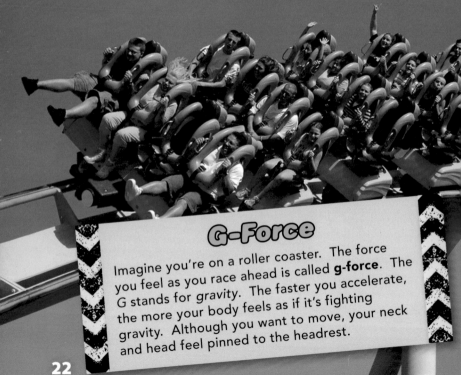

G-Force

Imagine you're on a roller coaster. The force you feel as you race ahead is called **g-force**. The G stands for *gravity*. The faster you accelerate, the more your body feels as if it's fighting gravity. Although you want to move, your neck and head feel pinned to the headrest.

Pedal to the Metal

30 miles per hour to 60 miles per hour

The velocity is increasing, so the car is accelerating.

30 mph ——————————————→ 60 mph

turning at 60 miles per hour

The car is changing direction (velocity), so the car is accelerating even though its speed stays the same.

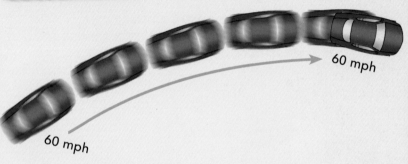

60 mph

60 mph

60 miles per hour to 0 miles per hour

The car is decelerating when the velocity is decreasing. This is negative acceleration.

60 mph ——————————————→ 0 mph

Newton's Second Law

Isaac Newton was a brilliant scientist who lived in the 17th century and used math to study the world around him. Later, other scientists studied his writings and created three laws of motion based on his work. Newton's Second Law of Motion relates to acceleration.

Acceleration occurs when a force acts on a **mass**. The greater the mass of the object being accelerated, the greater the amount of force needed to accelerate the object. This means that for something to speed up or slow down, it needs to have a force pushing or pulling it. It also says that the more mass an object has, the more force is needed to change its velocity. For example, it takes more force to move a bowling ball than a table-tennis ball.

The Newton

The unit of force used in physics is named after Sir Isaac Newton. A **newton (N)** is the force it takes to accelerate 1 kilogram (kg) 1 meter (m) per second (s) squared in empty space. For example, that means if a 1 kilogram bowling ball is pushed with 1 N of force, then 1 second later, the ball is moving $1\frac{m}{s}$. Two seconds later, it is moving $2\frac{m}{s}$, and so on.

$$N = kg\ \frac{m}{s^2}$$

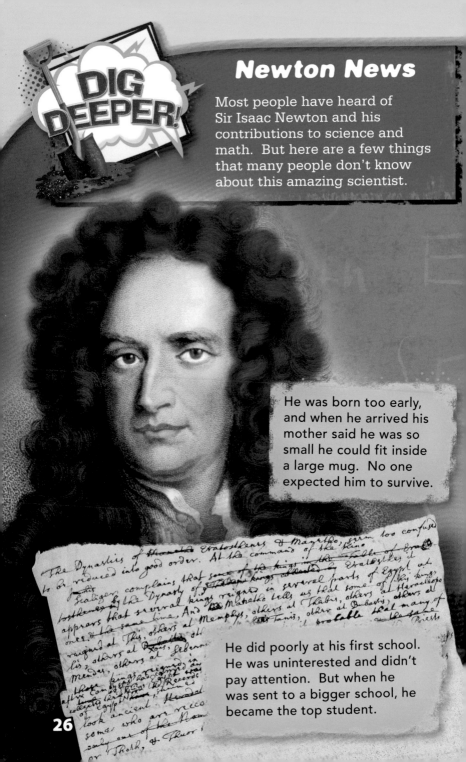

Newton News

Most people have heard of Sir Isaac Newton and his contributions to science and math. But here are a few things that many people don't know about this amazing scientist.

He was born too early, and when he arrived his mother said he was so small he could fit inside a large mug. No one expected him to survive.

He did poorly at his first school. He was uninterested and didn't pay attention. But when he was sent to a bigger school, he became the top student.

He invented calculus, a form of math, to help himself work out physics problems. But he was so shy about his work that he didn't tell anyone for 30 years!

He was elected to Parliament for a year, but in that time, he only uttered one sentence. He asked an assistant to close a drafty window.

Thrust

How do you get a cue ball moving fast? First, give it a tremendous push with the cue stick! Pushes that start something moving are called **thrust**. A little thrust might be a gentle push that gets you moving on a swing, or it might help you blow a bubble. And a big thrust might be powerful enough to launch a rocket! Whether the thrust is big or small, each push is using energy to get something moving in a particular direction.

On the Track

In a derby, racers are only allowed to use gravity to accelerate their model cars. But what if the rules changed? How could you use thrust to improve the speed of your car?

Take to the Sky

When birds flap their wings, they are using the force of thrust to stay in the air. Without thrust, a bird would crash to the ground. The larger they are, the more strength birds need to create a powerful thrust that keeps them safely in the air.

weight

drag

thrust

lift

Gravity

Not only does gravity keep us tied to Earth so we don't float away but it is also useful in getting things moving. A roller coaster uses a chain to pull the coaster up to the top of a tall hill, but after that, gravity takes over. The roller coaster races down toward Earth because gravity is pulling on it. In fact, there is so much force from gravity the roller coaster has enough energy to make it up the next hill and around the next curve. Then, it races down again and is pulled by the gravity of Earth. Roller coaster engineers understand exactly how each force pulls and pushes the ride from start to finish.

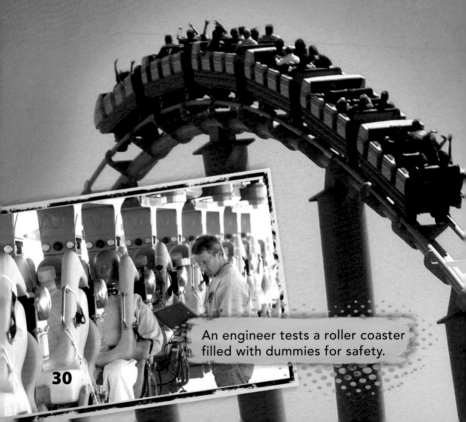

An engineer tests a roller coaster filled with dummies for safety.

Martian Gravity

Gravity is caused by the pull of mass. The planet Mars has less mass than Earth and only about 38 percent of the gravity on Earth. That means Mars pulls less on things. How would this affect the performance of a model race car? Would it change the outcome if the race were held on Mars?

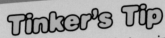

Tinker's Tip

Derby racers use gravity as their main force. Can you think of any way to increase the force of gravity on a model car? Most races allow participants to add weights to their cars. Does gluing weights on to the car change how the car races? Experiment a bit and see!

Magnetism

Have you ever played with magnets? Place one next to another on a table, and *zip*—the magnets slam together in the blink of an eye. **Magnetism** is another force that can change speed and velocity. Magnets are special materials that pull or push other magnetic things. Only certain metals have the right properties to become magnets. The most common metals are iron, steel, nickel, and cobalt. By using these materials, it's possible to create machines that can propel all kinds of objects very quickly.

Maglev Trains

Maglev stands for *magnetic levitation* and is a method for propelling trains. Magnets are used to create both lift and thrust, propelling a train along a track. The trains don't experience friction with the ground since they are floating! The fastest maglev trains can go 361 miles per hour. But there are currently only two maglev trains in operation. While maglev trains are being developed in Germany and Japan, the only one in operation is in China.

Find a pair of strong magnets, and attach one to the bottom of a toy car. Make sure the magnet doesn't keep the wheels from turning. Then, place your car on a raised track. Drag the second magnet under the track to pull your car. How far will the car roll once you pull the magnet away?

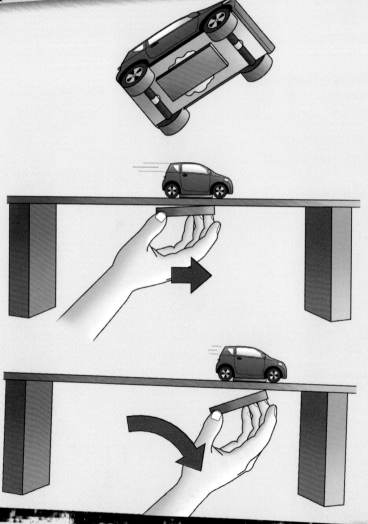

Keep It Going

One interesting thing to remember about speed is that things seem to want to keep going whatever speed and direction they are already going. That is, they will keep going the same speed unless something else actively changes the situation. It takes more energy to get something to change than it does to have it stay the same. This idea is called **inertia**. Inertia is the **resistance** to a change in motion.

Newton's First Law

Newton observed and described these facts, too. In fact, these observations were thought to be so basic and important they were written up as his First Law. Sometimes, this is called the Law of Inertia:

An object at rest will remain at rest unless acted on by an outside force. And an object in motion continues in motion with the same speed and direction unless acted on by an outside force.

A Never-Ending Race

Imagine placing your race car on a flat track. It won't move unless something makes it move. But if you gave it a giant push, it would start to roll and continue to roll unless something stopped it, such as wind, a hill, a small bump in the road, gravity, or something else that actively changed the situation. But if you pushed the car and nothing changed the situation, it would keep rolling, and rolling, and rolling due to inertia. It could participate in a never-ending race!

Gaining Momentum

Think of a ball rolling on the ground. If you tap it lightly with your finger, you can keep it rolling. Once the ball is on the move, it doesn't take much force because it has inertia. The moving ball also has **momentum**. Momentum is mass in motion.

Now, think of the same ball sitting still on the ground. If you tap it with the same light touch you used as when it was rolling, it may not move at all this time. That's because it takes more energy to get the ball to start rolling than it does to keep it rolling continuously. And it takes more energy to stop the ball from rolling than it does to keep it rolling once it has started!

Physics Formula

Where *p* is *momentum*, *m* is *mass* and *v* is *velocity*.

$$p = mv$$

Marble Madness

Momentum can be transferred from object to object. Check out the marbles hanging above. When the red ball hits the next ball, it will transfer its momentum. The red ball will hit the first silver ball; the first silver ball will hit the second; and the second will hit the third. As each marble hits the next, they build momentum. What do you think will happen if another ball is added to the line?

Egg Drop

In this experiment, you will see the forces of inertia and gravity at work. Pay close attention to the egg before it falls. Did it fall instantly? Why or why not? Can you think of another way to carry out the same experiment using different materials?

Materials:

- 1 large plastic drinking glass with an opening wide enough for an egg to fit through easily
- water
- 1 lightweight pie tin
- 1 empty toilet-paper roll
- 1 hard-boiled egg

Step 1

Fill the glass three-quarters full with water.

Step 2

Center the pie tin on the glass. Then, center the toilet paper tube on the pie tin. Balance the egg on the tube.

Step 3

Get an adult's permission before you do this next step. With a smooth, strong, horizontal motion, hit the pie plate so it flies away from the glass. If you do it correctly, the egg will plop into the glass with a neat splash!

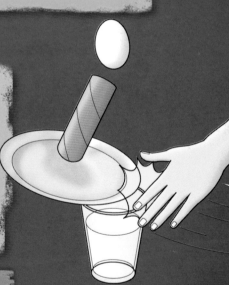

What's Happening Here?

The egg isn't moving when it's sitting on the tube. And when you smack the pie plate, no thrust is acting on the egg. Inertia keeps the egg at rest. But with no tube under it, of course, gravity pulls on the egg, so it falls straight down into the waiting cup.

Balancing Act

What does it mean for forces to be in balance? It means that nothing is changing. The amount something is pushing on an object in one direction is the same as the amount it is being pushed from the other direction. For instance, a boat that is floating in water is being pushed up by the **upthrust,** or buoyancy, of the water, but gravity is also pulling it down. What if the forces on the boat are unbalanced? If the force of gravity is greater than the force of upthrust, the boat will sink!

⇩ gravity

⇧ upthrust

Building Blocks

Just about everyone has played with building blocks at some time. Some like to stack them as high as they can, and others like to build imaginary kingdoms. But either way, the **balancing forces** are at work, keeping the pieces stacked in place. Gravity pushes down, but the blocks push up on each other. If you keep them balanced correctly, all the blocks will stay in place. Experiment a bit and see!

Slow It Down

Think of a tug-of-war game. One team pulls the rope in one direction while another team pulls the same rope in the other direction. If the teams are evenly matched, neither moves. The forces are in balance. But what if the second team just drops the rope and walks away? The first team would have no force to resist. It could run back as fast as it wanted with the rope. The **opposing force** was slowing it down, but when the other team let go, the force disappeared.

To make something go fast, you have to maximize forces that increase speed and minimize forces that work against speed. When you want to slow down or stop, the process is reversed. You need to minimize forces that are accelerating an object and maximize those that are decelerating it.

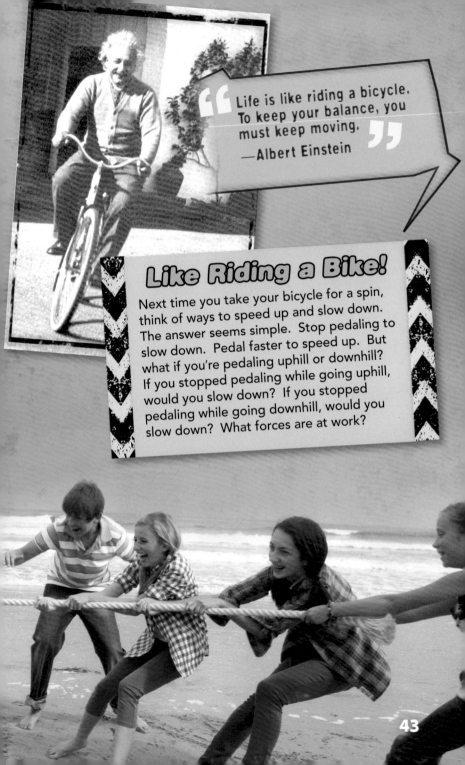

> **"** Life is like riding a bicycle. To keep your balance, you must keep moving. **"**
> —Albert Einstein

Like Riding a Bike!

Next time you take your bicycle for a spin, think of ways to speed up and slow down. The answer seems simple. Stop pedaling to slow down. Pedal faster to speed up. But what if you're pedaling uphill or downhill? If you stopped pedaling while going uphill, would you slow down? If you stopped pedaling while going downhill, would you slow down? What forces are at work?

Thrust, gravity, or magnetism will tend to slow you down if they are pushing or pulling the opposite way you are going. These are called *opposing forces*, but there is another force that comes into play, too. Friction is what happens when two materials rub together. It is a force that acts on surfaces, slowing things down or stopping them from moving.

In baseball, a race to the plate can be slowed by friction on the ground.

Forced Together

Think about spinning a top. What physical forces are at work? Tops stay upright as long as the forces at work are balanced. But eventually, the energy in the thrust that got the top spinning is spent. Friction slows the top down, and gravity pulls it to the ground.

Gravity pulls down on the top.

Thrust spins the top.

Friction slows the top as it comes in contact with the molecules in the air and those in the floor.

The floor pushes up on the top.

Match Up

Socks come in pairs. Twins come in pairs. Wings, arms, and eyes come in pairs. As it turns out, forces come in pairs, too! Whenever one force is applied to an object, another opposite force is also at work. These are called **action-reaction force pairs**. Newton's Third Law describes how they work. For every action, there is an equal (in size) and opposite (in direction) reaction. This is sometimes called *conservation of momentum*. If one object has momentum going in one direction, then another object receives equal momentum going the opposite way.

Feel the Force

Press your hand against the edge of a table. Notice how your hand gets bent out of shape. This is because a force is being exerted on it. You can see the edge of the table pressing into your hand. You can feel the table exerting a force on your hand. Now, try pressing harder. The harder you press, the harder the table pushes back. You can only feel the forces being exerted on you, not the forces you exert on something else. So when you push on the table, what you see and feel on your hand is the force the table exerts on you.

A Sporting Example

Think of a bat hitting a baseball. The bat swings to the left. The ball is coming from the right. When the bat hits the ball, the ball flies off to the left. But the bat is affected, too. It gets pushed back to the right.

Rub-a-dub-dub

Friction is a force that happens when things come in contact with each other. Most things are not perfectly smooth. They have little bits sticking out. They have texture to their surfaces. When they rub together, these little bits catch on each other and slow things down.

Oil can reduce friction in a bicycle and increase speed.

Hot! Hot! Hot!

Try rubbing your hands together quickly. In only a few seconds, you should start to notice them warming up. The little grooves in your skin catch on each other and create friction that changes energy into heat.

Tinker's Tip

Think about a model car again. Friction is the main force slowing it as it rolls down the ramp. So, how can you reduce the friction? First, you have to figure out where the friction is happening. In other words, what moving parts are touching? The wheels are touching the ramp. Try putting a lubricant like oil or graphite on the wheels. It will reduce friction and make your car go faster.

What a Drag

Not all friction happens between things with obvious bumps and grooves. Friction happens at a molecular level, too. Molecules bump and rub against each other. Think about walking into the wind. Wind is just air. It has no rough edges or grooves, but the air molecules push against you. They slow you down because they catch on the molecules in your skin. And they build up in front of you. The pull caused by the friction of a **fluid**, like air or water, is called resistance or **drag**. The force of air pushing against you is called **air resistance**.

An engineer inspects the blades of a wind tunnel.

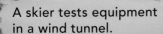

A skier tests equipment in a wind tunnel.

This model plane is being tested in a wind tunnel.

Wind Tunnel

How can engineers tell if air is moving smoothly around something? They use a wind tunnel. The tunnel has a fan at one end that blows air in a controlled stream. The object being tested is put in the middle. Then, smoke or fog is added to the air so engineers can see how it is flowing.

Water Resistance

Have you ever tried walking in a swimming pool? The water pushes back, and it's hard to go forward. But if you turn your body to face the floor and begin to swim, you move much more easily. The force of the water as you try to pass through it is **water resistance**. When you are walking on the bottom of the pool, your body is like a big flat box. You are pushing against the water, and the water has nowhere to go. It builds up in front of you and pushes back, but when you turn lengthwise to swim, suddenly there is much less water pushing in front of you. The water slips around you easily.

Streamlining

Engineers who design cars, boats, and airplanes spend a lot of time thinking about resistance. The process of reducing resistance on an object is called **streamlining**. The idea is to move through air or water or on land without getting caught on anything.

Engineers use computers to help them predict how products will behave in air or water.

Swimming Fast

Many competitive swimmers try to make their bodies as smooth as possible. Most wear swim caps to hold down their hair so it won't create drag. Some shave off body hair before a competition. Others wear special full-body swimsuits to keep themselves as smooth as possible while they swim!

Diving Down

In this experiment, you will determine which shapes are able to slip more quickly through a fluid and which are more affected by drag. What do you notice about the shapes that fell faster compared to those that were slower? Do your observations support what you have learned about streamlining and water resistance?

Materials:

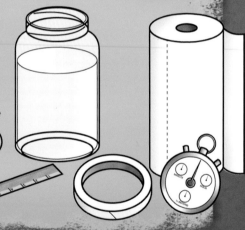

- 1 measuring stick
- 1 jar nearly filled with water
- masking tape
- 1 piece of modeling clay (roughly the size of a walnut)
- stopwatch
- paper towels

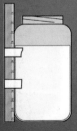

Step 1

Tape the measuring stick to the outside of the jar, leaving four inches remaining at the top. Make sure the stick is securely fastened. It shouldn't move during the experiment.

Step 2

Roll the modeling clay into a sphere. From the top of the measuring stick, drop the sphere into the water. Time how long it takes for the clay to reach the bottom of the jar.

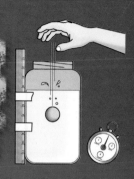

Step 3

Gently pat the clay dry with paper towels. Take care to not let the paper stick.

Step 4

Form the clay into a long oval. Drop the new shape into the water from the top of the measuring stick, and time its descent. Remove the clay, and gently pat it dry.

To Finish

Mold the clay into a cube, a star, a flat patty, or any other shape you can think of to repeat the test. Compare your observations of each shape. Decide which shape was slowest and which was fastest. List the shapes in order from slowest to fastest.

Full Speed Ahead

Nearly every roadway has a speed limit, so the speed we travel is not always up to us. But with a little knowledge of physics and plenty of energy, you can choose your own path, build up tons of momentum, and accelerate to the end of the world and back! So, experiment to find out what will take you where you want to go, and where you'll stop, no one knows!

Tinker's Tip

If something doesn't go as fast as you want it to the first time, start asking questions. Break down the motion into steps to see where you might improve the system. Then, try it again!

Speed Limits Around the World

Australia
110 mph

New Zealand
62 mph

United States
85 mph

China
75 mph

United Kingdom
70 mph

acceleration—the rate of change of velocity; speeding up or changing direction

action-reaction force pairs—pairs of forces that result from Newton's Third Law that states for every action, there is an equal and opposite reaction.

air resistance—the friction created as air moves past an object

axle—a fixed bar or beam on which wheels revolve

balancing forces—forces that act on each other in such a way that no change occurs

deceleration—the rate of change of velocity; slowing down or changing direction

drag—the force that acts against the motion of an object

energy—the ability to do work

exerting—putting forth

fluid—matter that has the ability to pour or flow

friction—the force that acts on surfaces in contact and slows them down or stops them from moving

g-force—the gravitational force; the force you feel when you accelerate

gravity—the pull of any object with mass

inertia—the tendency of an object to maintain its state of motion; moving things keep moving, still things stay still

kinetic energy—energy of movement

magnetism—a force that exists between special kinds of metals

mass—amount of matter something is made of

momentum—mass in motion

newton (N)—a unit used to measure force; the force it takes to move one kilogram one meter per second squared in empty space

opposing force—a force pushing or pulling in the opposite direction of another force

physicists—people who study the underlying rules of the universe, matter, and energy

potential energy—energy that is stored or results from position

relative—exists in comparison to something else

resistance—another word for *drag*; friction from a fluid

speed—change in position over time

streamlining—the process of reducing resistance

thrust—a push that gets something moving

traction—the friction of a body on a surface as it moves

upthrust—a sudden and forceful upward movement

velocity—speed in a certain direction

water resistance—the friction of water as it passes around an object

Index

Bibliography

Lepora, Nathan. *High-Speed Thrills: Acceleration and Velocity (Theme Park Science).* **Ticktock Media Limited, 2008.**

A theme park is the ideal place to see science in action. This book explains concepts such as force, acceleration, motion, and more, using exciting thrill rides found at amusement parks.

Spilsbury, Richard. *Speed and Acceleration (Fantastic Forces).* **Heinemann-Raintree, 2006.**

What's the fastest running animal on Earth? What happens when bumper cars crash? This book asks the questions you'll want answered about speed and acceleration. Charts, graphs, and hands-on experiments help bring science to life.

Sullivan, Navin. *Speed (Measure Up!).* **Benchmark Books, 2006.**

Learn about velocity, reaction speed, buoyancy, and gravity. Perform at-home experiments to see how familiar objects measure up.

VanCleave, Janice. *Physics for Every Kid: 101 Easy Experiments in Motion, Heat, Light, Machines, and Sound (Science for Every Kids Series).* **Wiley, 1991.**

Have you ever wondered what makes a curve ball curve or how magnets work? Basic physics principles are explored in these experiments. Each includes a list of materials, step-by-step instructions, the expected results, and an easy-to-understand explanation.

More to Explore

PBS Kids Physics Games

http://pbskids.org/games/physics.html

Explore the effects of friction, gravity, momentum, and other properties of physics while solving puzzles with PBS characters.

Exploratorium: Sports Science

http://www.exploratorium.edu/explore/staff_picks/sports_science/

This online museum of science features multiple web pages for investigating the different principles of physics found in sports. Some sports included are hockey, baseball, and skateboarding.

Physics Games.Net

http://www.physicsgames.net/

This is a collection of online physics-based games. Players won't even realize they're learning more about physics properties as they solve puzzles and play games.

NASA for Students

http://www.nasa.gov/audience/forstudents/index.html

Find the appropriate grade level to research interesting articles, images, and videos that show how NASA uses the Laws of Motion to plan space flights.

About the Author

Stephanie Paris is a seventh-generation Californian. She has her Bachelor of Arts in psychology from University of California, Santa Cruz, and her multiple-subject teaching credential from California State University, San Jose. She has been an elementary classroom teacher, an elementary school computer and technology teacher, a home-schooling mother, an educational activist, an educational author, a web designer, a blogger, and a Girl Scout leader. Ms. Paris lives in Germany, where she occasionally likes to drive fast on the Autobahn!